The Loudest Sneeze

Written by Jenny Feely
Illustrated by Chantal Stewart

2

My grandpa has the loudest sneeze you've ever heard. Grandma says you can hear it from two streets away.

If Grandpa is close by, you nearly jump out of your skin when he sneezes.

Any sort of yellow flowers
make Grandpa sneeze.

If he smells a yellow flower, he sneezes.
If he even sees a yellow flower, he sneezes.

No one on our street grows yellow flowers.
No one would dare!
It's too scary when he sneezes.

5

Everyone teases Grandpa
about his sneezes.

"Don't worry about that," he says.
"It's a sneeze to be proud of, and
I'm sure it will come in handy one day."

One day, we went on a picnic
in the country. We were having
a great time.

Then Grandpa said,
"Where's Grandma?"

We looked and looked for her.
We called, "Grandma! Grandma!"
But we couldn't find her anywhere.

We were very worried.

Then Grandpa walked past a plant
with yellow flowers on it.
He began to sneeze.
He sneezed and sneezed and sneezed.

"Aaaaaaaaaaachoooooooo!"
The sneezes were so big and so loud,
they almost blew us away.

14

All of a sudden, we saw Grandma
walking toward us.

"There you are!" said Grandma.

"Where have you been? We've been
looking for you everywhere!" we all cried.

"I was lost," said Grandma. "Then I heard
Grandpa sneezing, so I followed
the sneezes until I found you."

15

Grandpa just smiled and said,
"See? I told you that one day
my sneeze would come in handy!"